Divine

Pedagogy

Divine

Pedagogy

*A Guide for Writing
Your Philosophy of
Christian Education*

Dr. R. C. Titus

Copyright © 2024 R. C. Titus. All rights reserved.

No part of this book may be reproduced, stored in a retrieval system, or transmitted in any form or by any means, electronic, mechanical, photocopying, recording, or otherwise, without the prior written permission of the publisher.

Published by Wayfinder Education

Email: ron.titus@wayfinderacademy.org

Library of Congress
Cataloging-in-Publication Data is Available:

ISBN: 979-8328468695 (hardcover)
ISBN: 979-8328619059 (paperback)

Printed in the United States of America

Contents

Preface xv

    The Author xix

    About Wayfinder xxi

Chapter 1: The Heart of Christian Education ... 1

    Living Out Our Faith in the Classroom 1

    Embodying Christian Educational Philosophy 2

    Setting the Educational Environment 3

    Curriculum Design and Integration 4

    Pedagogical Approaches 5

    Building Relationships and Mentorship 6

    Engaging with the Broader Community 7

Chapter 2: Theological Foundation 9

Anchoring in Truth 9

Understanding Biblical Principles 10

Integrating Theology into Curriculum Design ... 10

Modeling Christian Worldview in Pedagogy 11

Classrooms that Reflects Christian Values 12

Engaging with Students on a Spiritual Level........ 13

In Conclusion 14

Chapter 3: Historical Perspectives 17

Walking Through the Pages of History 17

The Early Church: A Foundation of Faith 18

The Middle Ages: The Rise of Monastic Education
.... 18

The Reformation: A Renewed Focus on Scripture
.... 19

The Enlightenment: Tension Between Faith and Reason 20

The Modern Era: The Challenge of Secularization
.... 21

Contemporary Movements: A Renewed Vision . 21

Conclusion: A Legacy of Faith 22

Chapter 4: Worldview Analysis 25

Discerning Truth in a Tapestry of Beliefs 25

Embracing the Christian Worldview 26

Comparing Worldviews with Clarity and Compassion 26

Analyzing Worldviews Across Disciplines 27

Engaging with Contemporary Issues 28

Nurturing a Reflective and Discerning Spirit 29

In Conclusion 29

Chapter 5: Practical Application 31

Living Out Our Faith in Education 31

Breathing Life into Curriculum Content 32

Teaching Methods That Reflect Christ's Love ... 33

Creating Classrooms as Communities of Grace .. 33

Fostering Critical Thinking Through a Biblical Lens...34

Walking Alongside Students in Their Spiritual Journey 35

In Conclusion 35

Chapter 6: Critical Engagement 37

Navigating Culture with Faith 37

Critical Thinking within a Christian Framework 38

Engaging with Contemporary Issues Through Faith 38

Analyzing Worldviews in Various Disciplines.....39

Encouraging Respectful Dialogue and Debate....40

Applying Faith to Modern Dilemmas and Decisions 40

In Conclusion 41

Chapter 7: Personal Reflection and Development 43

Growing in Grace and Knowledge.......................43

Embarking on a Journey of Self-Reflection 44

Integrating Reflection into Our Professional Practice 44

Cultivating a Philosophy of Education 45

Engaging with Students on a Deeper Level 46

Fostering a Community of Reflective Practitioners 47

In Conclusion 47

Chapter 8: Community and Service 49

Extending Grace Beyond the Classroom 49

Cultivating a Classroom Community of Grace ... 50

Integrating Service Learning with Heart and Mind 50

Fostering a Spirit of Volunteerism 51

Engaging Global Concerns through a Christian Lens................. 52

Building a Culture of Giving and Generosity 52

In Conclusion 53

Chapter 9: Implementing the Philosophy..........55

Walking the Talk in Educational Settings............55

Embracing and Living Out Our Educational Philosophy..56

Curriculum as a Reflection of Faith.....................56

Pedagogy That Mirrors Christian Values............57

Building a Reflective Practice 58

Fostering Community Engagement.....................58

In Conclusion 59

Chapter 10: Growth as a Disciplined Practice..61

A Journey of Continuous Improvement.............61

Embracing Reflection as a Catalyst for Growth..62

The Evolving Nature of Our Educational Philosophy..62

Deepening Our Engagement with Students 63

The Ripple Effect of Our Professional Growth ..63

Looking Forward with Hope and Determination 64

In Conclusion 65

Sharing Your Philosophy 67

Writing Your Philosophy of Christian Education Paper 67

Preface

I often refer to pedagogy as the art and science of teaching, it forms the foundation of our educational endeavors. As Christian educators, we commit to a distinctively Christian approach, one that goes beyond the mere transmission of knowledge to the profound task of shaping souls and nurturing a deep-rooted faith capable of withstanding the challenges of our time. This journey is monumental yet profoundly beautiful, as it allows us to weave the timeless truths of the Christian faith into the very fabric of our educational practices.

Imagine stepping into a classroom where the walls resonate with more than just the echoes of academic discourse but with the whispers of a deeper calling. Here, lessons extend beyond the pages of textbooks to touch upon the eternal, where equations and essays serve as conduits for divine wisdom. This is the vision that propels us, the foundation upon which we build our educational edifice.

As you delve into this book, consider it a companion on your journey, offering guidance, inspiration, and practical wisdom for integrating Christian philosophy into every facet of your educational practice. You are not alone in this endeavor. Across the globe, countless educators are united in this sacred mission, each contributing to a tapestry of learning that glorifies God and enriches humanity.

Now, imagine the transformative power of a classroom where each lesson is infused with faith, where students are not only learners but seekers, embarking on a quest to find God in the midst of algebra, history, and literature. Envision a curriculum that does more than inform—it transforms, presenting every subject through the lens of Christian truth.

Consider the impact of teaching methods that mirror the values of the Gospel, where love, patience, respect, and empathy are not mere ideals but lived realities. Picture a classroom environment that reflects the Christian community, a sanctuary of learning where every student feels valued, understood, and inspired.

As educators, our role extends beyond the academic; we are mentors, guides, and at times, spiritual shepherds. Our interactions with students offer profound opportunities to influence their hearts and minds, to plant seeds of faith that will grow and flourish in God's timing.

In the following pages, you will find a mosaic of strategies, stories, and reflections aimed at equipping you to weave your faith into the very fabric of your educational practice. From curriculum development to classroom management, from pedagogical approaches to personal reflections, this book is designed to support you in your mission to educate, inspire, and transform.

Let us step forward with courage and conviction, embracing our calling as Christian educators. Together, we can create an educational experience that not only enlightens the mind but also ignites the soul, preparing our students to live out their faith with integrity, wisdom, and compassion in a world that desperately needs their light.

To maximize your engagement with this book and deepen your understanding of Christian education, I encourage you to respond to the writing prompts provided at the end of each chapter. These prompts are designed to facilitate personal reflection and practical application of the principles discussed. I recommend maintaining a reflective journal as you progress through the book, recording your responses and any additional insights or questions that arise. This journal can serve as a valuable resource for your ongoing professional development and spiritual growth.

In His Service,

Dr. Ronald C. Titus

The Author

Dr. R. C. Titus is the founder and CEO of Wayfinder Education, an accomplished educator, leader, and coach dedicated to fostering emotional resilience and integrating faith into education. Raised in North Platte, Nebraska, in a hardworking family of six children, he learned perseverance and resourcefulness from his parents and grandparents. These early experiences shaped his holistic approach to education.

Currently, Dr. Titus serves as the Chair of the School of Education and Director of a Lab School at a Southern Nazarene University. As a Professor of Educational Psychology, he integrates educational psychological theory, project-based learning, and social-emotional learning into a holistic classroom approach. He emphasizes mastery, autonomy, and purpose in lifelong learning through research-based strategies for student and teacher well-being and growth.

Dr. Titus's innovative Christian leadership has contributed to strong, healthy, and growing organizations. He offers strategies that blend faith with positive psychological principles to promote emotional well-being and organizational flourishing. An advocate for students with special needs and a strong supporter of school choice, Dr. Titus champions diverse learning environments tailored to meet the unique needs of all students. He is passionate about experiential learning, encouraging schools to integrate project-based learning and social-emotional learning skills, believing these settings provide opportunities to grasp the poetic knowledge described by Aristotle and St. Thomas Aquinas.

Beyond his professional interests, Dr. Titus enjoys reading, writing music, and exploring new technologies. His favorite verse, Romans 12:2, reflects his commitment to transformation and renewal: "Do not conform to the pattern of this world, but be transformed by the renewing of your mind. Then you will be able to test and approve what God's will is—his good, pleasing and perfect will."

About Wayfinder

Wayfinder Education seeks to help guide individuals in the pursuit of truth, inspired by the belief that God is the Waymaker and that through Him all things are possible. This distinctively Christian organization is dedicated to empowering individuals to live their best lives through a holistic approach to personal development and life coaching. By focusing on social and emotional learning along with practical life skills, Wayfinder Education aims to support personal growth and fulfillment.

Wayfinder Education provides a comprehensive range of life skills courses designed to equip individuals with essential competencies for personal and professional success. These courses focus on enhancing self-awareness, emotional intelligence, critical thinking, effective communication, financial literacy, and time management. By developing these skills, individuals are better equipped to experience human flourishing and lead fulfilling lives.

Wayfinder Education also provides free assessments to help individuals understand their strengths and areas for growth. These assessments include evaluations of emotional intelligence, personality traits, and leadership qualities, offering valuable insights for personal development.

Wayfinder Education adopts a holistic and practical approach to education. Courses are meticulously designed with expert insights and practical applications, ensuring that learners can apply their skills in real-world scenarios. Emphasizing continuous improvement, Wayfinder Education encourages a mindset of lifelong learning and personal growth.

Wayfinder Education is committed to providing high-quality, affordable life coaching and comprehensive life skills education grounded in Christian principles. By focusing on accessible coaching and practical, holistic education, Wayfinder Education helps individuals achieve personal and professional growth, leading to a more balanced and fulfilling life.

For more detailed information, you can visit the official website at www.wayfinderacademy.org.

Chapter 1: The Heart of Christian Education

Living Out Our Faith in the Classroom

In the bustling world of education, where facts and figures often take center stage, we are invited to pause and consider a deeper dimension of our calling as educators. Just as Jesus taught in parables, reaching the hearts of His listeners through stories and illustrations, we too are called to teach in a manner that transcends the mere transmission of information, engaging the very souls of our students.

"In the same way, let your light shine before others, that they may see your good deeds and glorify your Father in heaven" (Matthew 5:16). Imagine walking into a classroom where the air is thick with the presence of purpose and passion, where every lesson plan and classroom interaction is imbued with the essence of

Christian faith. This is the heart of Christian education—where the sacred and the secular are not segregated but seamlessly interwoven.

Embodying Christian Educational Philosophy

As educators, our first step is to internalize the philosophy we wish to impart. Just as a plant needs deep roots to withstand storms, our teaching must be deeply rooted in the fertile soil of Christian conviction. "For in him all things were created: things in heaven and on earth, visible and invisible, whether thrones or powers or rulers or authorities; all things have been created through him and for him. He is before all things, and in him all things hold together" (Colossians 1:16-17). This verse shapes our worldview, helping us understand that every part of the universe was created through and for Christ.

When teaching science, this perspective transforms the study of DNA from mere biological processes to a divine tapestry intricately woven by our Creator. Discussing the cosmos in an astronomy lesson becomes an exploration of God's vast and wondrous creation, where every star declares His glory (Psalm 19:1).

Setting the Educational Environment

With our philosophy firmly in place, we turn our attention to the environment we cultivate. Imagine a classroom that serves as a sanctuary, a place where students feel valued, respected, and loved—a reflection of Christ's love for us. In this sanctuary, the walls don't just hold educational posters and student artwork; they hold the echoes of encouragement, the whispers of prayers, and the residue of respectful, meaningful interactions.

"People were bringing little children to Jesus for him to place his hands on them, but the disciples rebuked them. When Jesus saw this, he was indignant. He said to them, 'Let the little children come to me, and do not hinder them, for the kingdom of God belongs to such as these. Truly I tell you, anyone who will not receive the kingdom of God like a little child will never enter it.' And he took the children in his arms, placed his hands on them and blessed them" (Mark 10:13-16). This image can inspire us to create an environment where every child feels welcomed and cherished. Our classrooms should reflect the warmth and acceptance Jesus showed, fostering a sense of belonging and love.

Curriculum Design and Integration

As we design our curriculum, we weave threads of biblical truth into the fabric of each subject. "In the beginning, God created the heavens and the earth" (Genesis 1:1). In history, we see God's hand guiding nations; in science, His creativity unfurling in DNA spirals and galaxy swirls; in literature, the echoes of redemption in every hero's journey. Our curriculum is not just a collection of topics but a tapestry that, when viewed in its entirety, reflects the beauty and coherence of God's truth.

Joseph's story in Genesis, where he rose from slavery to become a leader in Egypt, offers a powerful example of faith and perseverance when teaching about resilience and leadership. In literature, the theme of redemption found in many classic and contemporary stories mirrors the ultimate redemption story in the Bible. By highlighting these connections, we help students see the overarching narrative of God's plan throughout various subjects.

Pedagogical Approaches

Our teaching methods, too, are an expression of our faith. "Jesus answered, 'Everyone who drinks this water will be thirsty again, but whoever drinks the water I give them will never thirst. Indeed, the water I give them will become in them a spring of water welling up to eternal life'" (John 4:13-14). We employ strategies that honor each student's God-given dignity and potential, fostering an environment where questions are welcomed, where learning is a shared journey, and where each success and failure is met with grace and understanding. We teach not just to inform but to transform, inviting students to discover their calling and cultivate their gifts in service to God and others.

Building Relationships and Mentorship

In the context of Christian education, relationships extend beyond the confines of the classroom. We are mentors, guides, and sometimes even spiritual confidants. "Don't let anyone look down on you because you are young, but set an example for the believers in speech, in conduct, in love, in faith and in purity. Until I come, devote yourself to the public reading of Scripture, to preaching and to teaching. Do not neglect your gift, which was given you through prophecy when the body of elders laid their hands on you. Be diligent in these matters; give yourself wholly to them, so that everyone may see your progress. Watch your life and doctrine closely. Persevere in them, because if you do, you will save both yourself and your hearers" (1 Timothy 4:12-16). We invest in our students, recognizing that education is as much about shaping character as it is about imparting knowledge. We share not just our intellectual expertise but our life experiences, modeling what it means to live a life of faith.

Engaging with the Broader Community

"And let us consider how we may spur one another on toward love and good deeds, not giving up meeting together, as some are in the habit of doing, but encouraging one another—and all the more as you see the Day approaching" (Hebrews 10:24-25). We acknowledge that our classroom is not an island. We are part of a larger community—a tapestry of families, churches, and civic organizations. We seek partnerships and opportunities for our students to serve and engage, to see firsthand how their learning connects to the larger world and how they can be agents of change and ambassadors of Christ's love.

Engaging with the broader community helps students understand their role within the larger body of Christ and encourages them to live out their faith in practical ways.

In embracing this comprehensive approach to education, we embark on a sacred journey, one that challenges us to be both learners and teachers, shepherds and servants. We are crafting more than just lesson plans; we are nurturing hearts and minds to engage the world with the love and wisdom of Christ. This, dear educators, is our noble calling.

Writing Prompt for "Veritology: The Heart of Christian Education" Section of Your Philosophy of Christian Education Paper:

Reflect on the core principles of Christian education and how they align with your personal educational philosophy. Discuss how these principles shape your approach to teaching and learning. Describe ways you can more deeply integrate your faith into your educational practices.

Chapter 2: Theological Foundation

Anchoring in Truth

In the quest to impart wisdom and knowledge, we as educators are beckoned to anchor our teachings in the profound depths of theological truth. The Christian faith is not a mere addendum to our curriculum or a decorative mantlepiece in the classroom; it is the bedrock upon which all learning stands, offering a lens through which every subject comes into clearer focus.

"Sanctify them by the truth; your word is truth" (John 17:17). Our journey into integrating faith and education begins with a deep dive into Scripture, allowing God's Word to illuminate and guide our teaching philosophy. Understanding that truth is found in God's Word transforms our approach to education, making it a pursuit of understanding and living out divine truth.

Understanding Biblical Principles

"All Scripture is God-breathed and is useful for teaching, rebuking, correcting and training in righteousness, so that the servant of God may be thoroughly equipped for every good work" (2 Timothy 3:16-17). Our journey into integrating faith and education begins with a deep dive into Scripture, allowing God's Word to illuminate and guide our teaching philosophy. Understanding that all Scripture is inspired by God and beneficial for teaching helps us use the Bible as a foundation for all aspects of education.

Integrating Theology into Curriculum Design

With these foundational truths resonating in our hearts, we approach curriculum design with a renewed perspective. "In the beginning God created the heavens and the earth" (Genesis 1:1). We begin to see opportunities to weave theological insights across disciplines. In history, we trace God's providential hand through the ages; in literature, we uncover themes of redemption and sacrifice; in mathematics and science, we marvel at the order and complexity of God's creation.

For instance, when teaching about the creation of the universe, we can refer to Genesis 1:1, "In the beginning God created the heavens and the earth." This not only grounds the scientific study of the cosmos in a theological context but also invites students to see science as a way to explore and appreciate God's handiwork.

Modeling Christian Worldview in Pedagogy

"Jesus replied: 'Love the Lord your God with all your heart and with all your soul and with all your mind. This is the first and greatest commandment. And the second is like it: Love your neighbor as yourself'" (Matthew 22:37-39). Our teaching methods themselves become a reflection of our theological convictions. We foster classrooms that resonate with the love, grace, and truth of the Gospel. Discussions are infused with a spirit of humility and respect, reflecting the Christian call to love our neighbors as ourselves. We encourage critical thinking, not as an end in itself but as a means to discern truth, always pointing students back to the ultimate source of all wisdom.

Classrooms that Reflects Christian Values

"But the fruit of the Spirit is love, joy, peace, forbearance, kindness, goodness, faithfulness, gentleness and self-control. Against such things there is no law" (Galatians 5:22-23). Just as a church is more than a building, a classroom is more than a space for learning—it is a community where values are lived and nurtured. We strive to create an environment that reflects the fruits of the Spirit. In this setting, students are not only taught but are truly seen and valued, empowered to grow not just intellectually but spiritually and morally.

In the story of the Good Samaritan (Luke 10:25-37), Jesus illustrates the importance of compassion and kindness. This story can inspire us to create a classroom environment where every student feels cared for and supported, regardless of their background or circumstances.

Engaging with Students on a Spiritual Level

"If any of you lacks wisdom, you should ask God, who gives generously to all without finding fault, and it will be given to you" (James 1:5). In the rhythm of our academic year, we find moments to engage with students on a deeper spiritual level. This might mean pausing the lesson plan to address a heart issue, offering a word of encouragement, or sharing a personal testimony. It's in these moments that education transcends the acquisition of knowledge and becomes a transformative experience, shaping not only minds but hearts and souls.

Consider the story of Jesus and Zacchaeus in Luke 19:1-10. When Jesus saw Zacchaeus in the tree, He called him by name, and transformed his life through a personal encounter. Similarly, our interactions with students can have a profound impact when we take the time to see them, understand their struggles, and speak into their lives with love and truth.

In Conclusion

"Now may the God of peace, who through the blood of the eternal covenant brought back from the dead our Lord Jesus, that great Shepherd of the sheep, equip you with everything good for doing his will, and may he work in us what is pleasing to him, through Jesus Christ, to whom be glory for ever and ever. Amen" (Hebrews 13:20-21). As we endeavor to lay a theological foundation in our educational practice, we embark on a sacred calling. It is a calling to not only teach but to inspire, to not merely inform but to transform. We are not just educators; we are stewards of a profound truth, tasked with the privilege of guiding the next generation into a deeper understanding of the world and their place in it, all under the sovereignty of God.

In this endeavor, let us be diligent, let us be faithful, and above all, let us be prayerful, trusting that the One who calls us is faithful to complete the work He has begun in us and through us.

Writing Prompt for "Theology: My Theological Perspective" Section of Your Philosophy of Christian Education Paper:

Explore the theological foundations of your educational philosophy. How do biblical principles such as Colossians 1:16-17 and Matthew 6:33 influence your approach to teaching and curriculum design?

Chapter 3: Historical Perspectives

Walking Through the Pages of History

"For everything that was written in the past was written to teach us, so that through the endurance taught in the Scriptures and the encouragement they provide we might have hope" (Romans 15:4). As we journey through the landscape of Christian education, it becomes imperative to cast our gaze backward to learn from the vast expanse of history that precedes us. The story of Christianity is not confined to the realm of personal faith or church life; it has been a vibrant thread woven through the fabric of cultures, influencing art, science, governance, and indeed education itself. This chapter delves into these historical narratives, drawing lessons and inspiration for our educational endeavors today.

The Early Church: A Foundation of Faith

"Just as a body, though one, has many parts, but all its many parts form one body, so it is with Christ. For we were all baptized by one Spirit so as to form one body—whether Jews or Gentiles, slave or free—and we were all given the one Spirit to drink. Even so the body is not made up of one part but of many" (1 Corinthians 12:12-14). The early church laid the foundation for Christian education by fostering a sense of community and unity among believers. Early Christians gathered not only for worship but also for learning, sharing their knowledge and faith. This period set a precedent for integrating faith and learning, highlighting the importance of educating believers in the tenets of Christianity while nurturing a strong, supportive community.

The Middle Ages: The Rise of Monastic Education

"Indeed, if you call out for insight and cry aloud for understanding, and if you look for it as for silver and search for it as for hidden treasure, then you will understand the fear of the Lord and find the knowledge of God" (Proverbs 2:3-5). During the Middle Ages, monastic schools became centers of learning and scholarship. Monks dedicated themselves to the pursuit of knowledge, preserving classical texts and advancing theological studies. These monastic schools emphasized the search for divine wisdom and understanding, intertwining academic pursuits with spiritual growth. This era illustrates the profound impact of disciplined study and the integration of faith with rigorous intellectual inquiry.

The Reformation: A Renewed Focus on Scripture

"All Scripture is God-breathed and is useful for teaching, rebuking, correcting and training in righteousness, so that the servant of God may be thoroughly equipped for every good work" (2 Timothy 3:16-17). The Reformation brought a renewed emphasis on the authority of Scripture, transforming Christian education. Reformers like

Martin Luther and John Calvin advocated for widespread literacy and access to the Bible, ensuring that every believer could read and understand God's Word. This movement underscored the importance of grounding education in Scripture, equipping believers with the knowledge and discernment to live out their faith.

The Enlightenment: Tension Between Faith and Reason

"See to it that no one takes you captive through hollow and deceptive philosophy, which depends on human tradition and the elemental spiritual forces of this world rather than on Christ" (Colossians 2:8). The Enlightenment introduced new ways of thinking that often placed reason and empirical evidence above faith. This period created a tension between faith and reason, challenging Christians to reconcile their beliefs with emerging scientific and philosophical ideas. It was a time of robust debate and reflection, prompting Christian educators to defend and articulate their faith in the face of changing intellectual landscapes.

The Modern Era: The Challenge of Secularization

"Do not conform to the pattern of this world, but be transformed by the renewing of your mind. Then you will be able to test and approve what God's will is—his good, pleasing and perfect will" (Romans 12:2). The modern era brought about the rise of secularization, posing significant challenges to Christian education. As societies became more secular, the influence of Christianity in public education diminished. Christian educators were called to reaffirm their commitment to teaching from a biblical worldview, resisting the pressures to conform to secular norms and philosophies. This era highlights the importance of renewing one's mind and staying true to God's will amidst a shifting cultural landscape.

Contemporary Movements: A Renewed Vision

"What we have received is not the spirit of the world, but the Spirit who is from God, so that we may understand what God has freely given us. This is what we speak, not in words taught us by human wisdom but in words taught by the Spirit, explaining spiritual realities with Spirit-taught words" (1 Corinthians 2:12-13). Today, Christian education continues to evolve, embracing new methods and technologies while maintaining a steadfast commitment to biblical truth. Contemporary movements in Christian education emphasize holistic development, integrating spiritual, intellectual, and emotional growth. There is a renewed vision for creating learning environments that are deeply rooted in faith, driven by the Spirit, and responsive to the needs of the modern world.

Conclusion: A Legacy of Faith

"Therefore, since we are surrounded by such a great cloud of witnesses, let us throw off everything that hinders and the sin that so easily entangles. And let us run with perseverance the race marked out for us, fixing our eyes on Jesus, the pioneer and perfecter of faith" (Hebrews 12:1-2). As we reflect on the rich history of Christian education, we are reminded of the legacy of faith passed down through generations. This heritage encourages us to persevere in our calling as educators, continually seeking to honor God through our teaching. By fixing our eyes on Jesus, we are inspired to carry forward this legacy, nurturing the next generation of believers with wisdom, integrity, and a deep commitment to the truth of the Gospel.

Writing Prompt for "History: The Christian Narrative" Section of Your Philosophy of Christian Education Paper:

Examine the historical role of Christianity in shaping education. Identify key figures and movements that have influenced Christian education and discuss their impact on your own educational practice.

Chapter 4: Worldview Analysis

Discerning Truth in a Tapestry of Beliefs

"Jesus answered, 'I am the way and the truth and the life. No one comes to the Father except through me'" (John 14:6). In the vast marketplace of ideas where diverse worldviews clamor for attention, the task of discerning truth becomes both critical and complex. As Christian educators, we are called not only to impart knowledge but also to guide our students in understanding how a Christian worldview provides a coherent and meaningful interpretation of the world. This chapter explores how we can navigate this rich tapestry of beliefs, equipping our students with the tools to analyze, compare, and embrace a worldview rooted in the truth of the Gospel.

Embracing the Christian Worldview

"Do not conform to the pattern of this world, but be transformed by the renewing of your mind. Then you will be able to test and approve what God's will is—his good, pleasing and perfect will" (Romans 12:2). Our exploration begins by delving deep into the Christian worldview itself, understanding its foundational truths about God, humanity, and the cosmos. We immerse ourselves and our students in the narrative of Scripture, where we find the answers to life's ultimate questions: Who are we? Why are we here? What is wrong with the world, and how can it be fixed? In doing so, we offer not just a set of doctrines but an invitation to see the world through the lens of divine revelation.

Comparing Worldviews with Clarity and Compassion

"But in your hearts revere Christ as Lord. Always be prepared to give an answer to everyone who asks you to give the reason for the hope that you have. But do this with gentleness and respect" (1 Peter 3:15). With a firm grasp of our own worldview, we then venture out to understand others, approaching this task with both clarity and compassion. We teach our students to listen respectfully to different perspectives, to understand them accurately, and to engage in thoughtful dialogue. Our aim is not to defeat but to discern, not to argue but to illuminate, showing how the Christian worldview answers the deep longings and questions of the human heart with a coherence and completeness unmatched by any other.

Analyzing Worldviews Across Disciplines

"For in him all things were created: things in heaven and on earth, visible and invisible, whether thrones or powers or rulers or authorities; all things have been created through him and for him" (Colossians 1:16). This worldview analysis is not confined to religious or philosophical discussions alone; it permeates every academic discipline. In literature, we discern worldviews in the themes and motivations of characters; in science, we confront differing views on the origins and meaning of life; in history, we see the unfolding of worldviews in the rise and fall of civilizations. By weaving this analysis into our teaching, we help students see how a Christian worldview illuminates every area of inquiry, providing a framework for understanding the world that is both intellectually robust and deeply satisfying.

Engaging with Contemporary Issues

"He has shown you, O mortal, what is good. And what does the Lord require of you? To act justly and to love mercy and to walk humbly with your God" (Micah 6:8). Our journey of worldview analysis also engages with the pressing issues of our day, from ethical dilemmas in technology and medicine to debates over justice and human rights. Here we encourage our students to apply their Christian worldview not as a set of pat answers but as a dynamic, living faith that speaks to every aspect of life. We empower them to be thinkers and influencers, equipped to engage with the world's challenges with wisdom, compassion, and conviction.

Nurturing a Reflective and Discerning Spirit

"Finally, brothers and sisters, whatever is true, whatever is noble, whatever is right, whatever is pure, whatever is lovely, whatever is admirable—if anything is excellent or praiseworthy—think about such things" (Philippians 4:8). Finally, we cultivate in our students—and in ourselves—a spirit of reflection and discernment. In a world where new ideas and ideologies emerge daily, the ability to discern truth from error is indispensable. We encourage our students to be lifelong learners, continually deepening their understanding of their faith and how it applies to the world around them. We model this pursuit, demonstrating that the journey of understanding and applying a Christian worldview is a lifelong adventure, one that enriches our lives and equips us to be lights in the world.

In Conclusion

"The beginning of wisdom is this: Get wisdom. Though it cost all you have, get understanding"

(Proverbs 4:7). As we close this chapter, let us commit to being educators who do more than transmit information; let us be guides in the pursuit of truth, mentors in the journey of faith, and companions in the exploration of the world through the lens of Scripture. In doing so, we fulfill our calling not just to inform but to transform, preparing our students to navigate the complex world of ideas with confidence, conviction, and a deep-rooted faith.

Writing Prompt for "Anthropology: A Christian Worldview" Section of Your Philosophy of Christian Education Paper:

Analyze how a Christian worldview influences your understanding of humanity and the purpose of education. Compare this with other worldviews and discuss the implications for your teaching practice.

Chapter 5: Practical Application

Living Out Our Faith in Education

"Do not merely listen to the word, and so deceive yourselves. Do what it says" (James 1:22). In the realm of Christian education, understanding profound truths and historical insights lays a vital foundation, yet the true measure of our efforts is found in their application. How do we live out our faith through the vocation of teaching? This chapter seeks to journey with you through the practical outworking of a Christian educational philosophy, transforming classrooms into places where faith is not only taught but also caught and lived.

Breathing Life into Curriculum Content

"These commandments that I give you today are to be on your hearts. Impress them on your children. Talk about them when you sit at home and when you walk along the road, when you lie down and when you get up" (Deuteronomy 6:6-7). Imagine curriculum content as the canvas upon which we paint the colors of God's truth, where every subject is an opportunity to reflect His creativity, order, and wisdom. In literature, we find themes of redemption; in science, the intricacy of His design; in history, His sovereign hand. As educators, we weave these revelations into our lessons, showing students the interconnectedness of all knowledge under the lordship of Christ. This approach transforms learning from a mere acquisition of facts into an exploration of God's grand narrative, where every lesson resonates with purpose and meaning.

Teaching Methods That Reflect Christ's Love

"A new command I give you: Love one another. As I have loved you, so you must love one another. By this everyone will know that you are my disciples, if you love one another" (John 13:34-35). In the way we teach, we model the character of Christ, fostering classrooms that echo His patience, understanding, and love. Our pedagogical methods should not only convey information but also demonstrate grace, encouraging inquiry and promoting a spirit of mutual respect and dignity. We engage students not as vessels to be filled but as image-bearers to be nurtured, creating an environment where they feel valued, heard, and inspired to learn.

Creating Classrooms as Communities of Grace

"Be kind and compassionate to one another, forgiving each other, just as in Christ God forgave you" (Ephesians 4:32). Our classrooms should be sanctuaries of grace, where students experience a microcosm of the Christian community. Here, relationships are built on mutual respect and care, where successes are celebrated, and failures met with encouragement and the opportunity to grow. In this community, students learn to work together, support one another, and live out the 'one another' commands of Scripture, providing a tangible experience of Christian love in action.

Fostering Critical Thinking Through a Biblical Lens

"For the Lord gives wisdom; from his mouth come knowledge and understanding" (Proverbs 2:6). We are called to love God with all our minds, and this love involves rigorous thinking and discernment. We teach our students to engage critically with the world, analyzing ideas and issues through a biblical lens. This critical engagement is not for criticism's sake but to seek after truth, understanding the world more fully in light of God's Word. In doing so, we prepare our students to navigate the complexities of life with wisdom and discernment, equipped to make contributions that are thoughtful, edifying, and grounded in truth.

Walking Alongside Students in Their Spiritual Journey

"He is the one we proclaim, admonishing and teaching everyone with all wisdom, so that we may present everyone fully mature in Christ" (Colossians 1:28). As educators, our role extends beyond academic instruction; we are also mentors and guides in our students' spiritual journeys. We provide not only knowledge but also wisdom, not only lessons but also life application. Through our words and actions, we model a life of faith, available to counsel, encourage, and pray with our students, helping them to integrate their learning with their living.

In Conclusion

"Therefore encourage one another and build each other up, just as in fact you are doing" (1 Thessalonians 5:11). As we conclude this chapter, let us be encouraged and challenged to see our classrooms as fertile fields for faith to flourish. Our role as educators is a high calling, one that has eternal implications. By applying the principles of our Christian faith to every aspect of our teaching, we cultivate an environment where truth is discovered, lives are shaped, and hearts are turned toward God. Let us therefore approach our vocation with intentionality, creativity, and prayer, trusting that God will use our efforts to bear lasting fruit for His kingdom.

Writing Prompt for "Ethics and Praxis: Practical Application" Section of Your Philosophy of Christian Education Paper:

Detail how ethical principles derived from the Gospel guide your practical application of educational theories and practices. Provide examples from your teaching experience.

Chapter 6: Critical Engagement

Navigating Culture with Faith

"Do not conform to the pattern of this world, but be transformed by the renewing of your mind. Then you will be able to test and approve what God's will is—his good, pleasing and perfect will" (Romans 12:2). In a world where cultural currents can often pull us in directions contrary to our faith, it is imperative for Christian educators to guide students in navigating these waters with discernment and integrity. Our task is to transform minds through education that is deeply rooted in biblical principles, enabling students to critically engage with culture while remaining anchored in their faith.

Critical Thinking within a Christian Framework

"We demolish arguments and every pretension that sets itself up against the knowledge of God, and we take captive every thought to make it obedient to Christ" (2 Corinthians 10:5). Critical thinking is a crucial skill in today's complex world, yet for Christian educators, it goes beyond mere analysis and critique. It involves evaluating every idea and worldview against the truth of Scripture. By fostering an environment where questioning and thoughtful examination are encouraged, we help students develop the ability to discern truth and reject falsehood, ensuring their thoughts align with Christ's teachings.

Engaging with Contemporary Issues Through Faith

"He has shown you, O mortal, what is good. And what does the Lord require of you? To act justly and to love mercy and to walk humbly with your God" (Micah 6:8). Contemporary issues, from social justice to environmental concerns, present both challenges and opportunities for Christian education. We teach our students to engage these issues not just with academic rigor but with a heart of justice, mercy, and humility. By integrating faith with learning, we guide students to approach modern dilemmas with a Christ-centered perspective, emphasizing action that reflects God's character and commands.

Analyzing Worldviews in Various Disciplines

"Test all things; hold fast what is good" (1 Thessalonians 5:21). Every academic discipline, from science to humanities, offers a unique lens through which to view the world. In Christian education, we critically analyze these perspectives, affirming what aligns with biblical truth and challenging what does not. This process equips students to discern and hold fast to what is good, fostering a holistic understanding of how faith intersects with all areas of knowledge.

Encouraging Respectful Dialogue and Debate

"Let your conversation be always full of grace, seasoned with salt, so that you may know how to answer everyone" (Colossians 4:6). Respectful dialogue and debate are essential components of critical engagement. In our classrooms, we cultivate an atmosphere where students can express diverse viewpoints and engage in meaningful discussions with grace and respect. This approach not only enhances learning but also models how Christians can participate in broader societal conversations in a manner that reflects the love and wisdom of Christ.

Applying Faith to Modern Dilemmas and Decisions

"If any of you lacks wisdom, you should ask God, who gives generously to all without finding fault, and it will be given to you" (James 1:5). Modern dilemmas often require wisdom that transcends human understanding. As educators, we encourage our students to seek God's guidance in their decision-making processes. By teaching them to pray for wisdom and to rely on God's Word, we help them develop the confidence and discernment needed to navigate life's complexities with faith and integrity.

In Conclusion

"And this is my prayer: that your love may abound more and more in knowledge and depth of insight, so that you may be able to discern what is best and may be pure and blameless for the day of Christ" (Philippians 1:9-10). As we conclude this chapter, we are reminded of the importance of cultivating a love for truth, knowledge, and discernment in our students. By integrating faith with critical engagement, we prepare them to face the world with a well-rounded, biblically grounded perspective. Let us continue to encourage, challenge, and equip our students to be thoughtful, faithful, and discerning followers of Christ.

Writing Prompt for "Philosophy and Ethics: Critical Engagement" Section of Your Philosophy of Christian Education Paper:

Critically engage with contemporary educational philosophies and cultural issues through the lens of Christian ethics. Discuss how you integrate these insights into your teaching and interactions with students.

Chapter 7: Personal Reflection and Development

Growing in Grace and Knowledge

The journey of personal growth and development is central to the life of a Christian educator. As we nurture our students' intellectual and spiritual growth, we must also be committed to our own continuous development. "But grow in the grace and knowledge of our Lord and Savior Jesus Christ. To him be glory both now and forever! Amen" (2 Peter 3:18). This dual pursuit ensures that we are well-equipped to inspire and guide those entrusted to our care. Our growth in grace and knowledge reflects our commitment to the transformative power of Christ, shaping us into more effective and compassionate educators.

Embarking on a Journey of Self-Reflection

"Let us examine our ways and test them, and let us return to the Lord" (Lamentations 3:40). Self-reflection is a vital practice for educators who seek to align their lives and teaching with God's will. This introspective journey allows us to evaluate our actions, attitudes, and motivations, ensuring that they are consistent with our faith. By regularly examining our ways and testing them against the standards of Scripture, we open ourselves to the Holy Spirit's guidance, leading us back to the Lord and His purposes for our lives and vocations.

Integrating Reflection into Our Professional Practice

"Search me, God, and know my heart; test me and know my anxious thoughts. See if there is any offensive way in me, and lead me in the way everlasting" (Psalm 139:23-24). Integrating reflection into our professional practice involves inviting God into our hearts and classrooms. Through prayer and meditation on Scripture, we seek His insight into our teaching methods, relationships, and personal conduct. This process helps us identify areas for improvement and renewal, ensuring that our professional lives are a testament to our faith. By allowing God to search and know our hearts, we remain humble and open to His transformative work.

Cultivating a Philosophy of Education

"The beginning of wisdom is this: Get wisdom. Though it cost all you have, get understanding" (Proverbs 4:7). Developing a coherent philosophy of education rooted in Christian principles requires a dedication to acquiring wisdom and understanding. This pursuit is not merely academic but deeply spiritual, grounded in the belief that true wisdom comes from God. As we study educational theories and practices, we continually seek to integrate them with our faith, creating an educational approach that is both intellectually rigorous and spiritually enriching. This philosophy becomes the foundation upon which we build our teaching practices and interactions with students.

Engaging with Students on a Deeper Level

"He is the one we proclaim, admonishing and teaching everyone with all wisdom, so that we may present everyone fully mature in Christ" (Colossians 1:28). Engaging with students on a deeper level involves more than just imparting knowledge; it means walking alongside them in their spiritual journey. We proclaim Christ through our teaching, guiding students toward maturity in their faith. This engagement requires wisdom, patience, and a genuine investment in their personal and spiritual growth. By fostering meaningful relationships with our students, we help them integrate their faith with their learning, preparing them to live out their Christian convictions in every aspect of their lives.

Fostering a Community of Reflective Practitioners

"And let us consider how we may spur one another on toward love and good deeds, not giving up meeting together, as some are in the habit of doing, but encouraging one another—and all the more as you see the Day approaching" (Hebrews 10:24-25). Creating a community of reflective practitioners involves encouraging and supporting one another in our professional and spiritual journeys. By meeting regularly to share insights, challenges, and successes, we build a network of encouragement and accountability. This community fosters an environment where continuous improvement is valued, and where each member is spurred on to greater love and good deeds. Through collaboration and shared reflection, we grow together in our vocation as Christian educators.

In Conclusion

"Test all things; hold fast what is good" (1 Thessalonians 5:21). As we conclude this chapter, let us commit to a life of ongoing reflection and development. By testing our actions, attitudes, and practices against the truth of Scripture, we ensure that our work remains grounded in what is good and true. In holding fast to these principles, we honor God and enhance our effectiveness as educators. Let us strive to grow in grace and knowledge, continually seeking God's wisdom as we guide our students on their own journeys of faith and learning.

Writing Prompt for "Unio Mystica: Personal Reflection and Development" Section of Your Philosophy of Christian Education Paper:

Reflect on your personal growth and development as a Christian educator. How do spiritual practices and self-reflection enhance your effectiveness in the classroom?

Chapter 8: Community and Service

Extending Grace Beyond the Classroom

"The King will reply, 'Truly I tell you, whatever you did for one of the least of these brothers and sisters of mine, you did for me'" (Matthew 25:40). In the realm of Christian education, our mission extends far beyond the walls of the classroom. As educators, we are called to instill in our students a sense of compassion and responsibility towards others. This principle of extending grace and service is rooted in the words of Jesus, who taught that acts of kindness and service to the least among us are acts of love toward Him. By encouraging students to engage in acts of service, we help them understand the profound impact of living out their faith in tangible ways.

Cultivating a Classroom Community of Grace

"Be kind and compassionate to one another, forgiving each other, just as in Christ God forgave you" (Ephesians 4:32). Creating a classroom environment where grace and compassion thrive is essential for fostering a sense of community. This involves teaching students to practice kindness, forgiveness, and empathy towards one another. Such an environment not only enhances learning but also reflects the love and forgiveness we receive from Christ. By modeling and teaching these values, we build a supportive and nurturing community where every student feels valued and understood.

Integrating Service Learning with Heart and Mind

"In the same way, faith by itself, if it is not accompanied by action, is dead" (James 2:17). Service learning is an educational approach that integrates meaningful community service with instruction and reflection. It enriches the learning experience, teaches civic responsibility, and strengthens communities. By incorporating service learning into our curriculum, we connect students' academic learning with real-world applications, demonstrating that faith in action is vital. This holistic approach helps students develop a heart for service and a mind that seeks to address the needs of the world around them.

Fostering a Spirit of Volunteerism

"Each of you should use whatever gift you have received to serve others, as faithful stewards of God's grace in its various forms" (1 Peter 4:10). Encouraging students to volunteer and use their gifts for the benefit of others fosters a spirit of generosity and stewardship. By identifying and nurturing each student's unique talents, we guide them in finding ways to contribute meaningfully to their communities. This practice not only benefits those they serve but also helps students develop a deeper understanding of their own gifts and how they can be used for God's glory.

Engaging Global Concerns through a Christian Lens

"Therefore go and make disciples of all nations, baptizing them in the name of the Father and of the Son and of the Holy Spirit, and teaching them to obey everything I have commanded you. And surely I am with you always, to the very end of the age" (Matthew 28:19-20). In an increasingly interconnected world, it is crucial for students to engage with global issues from a Christian perspective. This involves educating them about international concerns such as poverty, injustice, and environmental sustainability, and encouraging them to respond with compassion and action. By framing these issues within the context of the Great Commission, we inspire students to see their role in God's global mission and to act as His ambassadors of hope and justice.

Building a Culture of Giving and Generosity

"Each of you should give what you have decided in your heart to give, not reluctantly or under compulsion, for God loves a cheerful giver" (2 Corinthians 9:7). Cultivating a culture of generosity within the school community involves more than just encouraging donations; it means fostering a spirit of joyful giving. By teaching students the value of generosity and providing opportunities for them to give their time, talents, and resources, we help them develop a habit of giving that reflects God's own generosity towards us. This culture of giving not only meets the needs of others but also enriches the givers, fostering a sense of fulfillment and joy.

In Conclusion

"Let us not become weary in doing good, for at the proper time we will reap a harvest if we do not give up" (Galatians 6:9). As we wrap up this chapter on community and service, we are reminded of the importance of perseverance in our efforts to do good. The seeds of service and generosity that we plant in our students' hearts will, in due time, bear fruit. By continually encouraging and equipping our students to serve others, we contribute to a legacy of faithfulness and compassion that will impact their lives and the world around them for generations to come.

Writing Prompt for "Sociology: Community and Service" Section of Your Philosophy of Christian Education Paper:

Propose a community service initiative that integrates Christian sociological principles. Discuss how this initiative fosters a sense of community and service among your students.

Chapter 9: Implementing the Philosophy

Walking the Talk in Educational Settings

"Do not merely listen to the word, and so deceive yourselves. Do what it says" (James 1:22). The true measure of our educational philosophy lies in its practical application. As Christian educators, we are called to embody the principles we teach, demonstrating our faith through our actions in the classroom and beyond. This involves more than just imparting knowledge; it requires living out our beliefs consistently and authentically. By doing so, we become credible witnesses to the transformative power of the Gospel, inspiring our students to integrate faith into every aspect of their lives.

Embracing and Living Out Our Educational Philosophy

"And whatever you do, whether in word or deed, do it all in the name of the Lord Jesus, giving thanks to God the Father through him" (Colossians 3:17). Embracing our educational philosophy means committing to a holistic approach where every word and action reflects our dedication to Christ. This comprehensive integration of faith and practice ensures that our teaching is not only informative but also transformative. By acknowledging Christ in all that we do, we create an environment where faith is naturally woven into the fabric of daily life, fostering a culture of gratitude and reverence.

Curriculum as a Reflection of Faith

"These commandments that I give you today are to be on your hearts. Impress them on your children. Talk about them when you sit at home and when you walk along the road, when you lie down and when you get up" (Deuteronomy 6:6-7). Our curriculum should serve as a living testament to our faith, embedding biblical principles throughout all subjects. This approach involves more than integrating scripture into lesson plans; it means shaping the entire educational experience to reflect God's truth and love. By doing so, we help students see the relevance of their faith in every area of study, guiding them to apply biblical principles in all aspects of their lives.

Pedagogy That Mirrors Christian Values

"Whatever you have learned or received or heard from me, or seen in me—put it into practice. And the God of peace will be with you" (Philippians 4:9). Our teaching methods should reflect the values of the Kingdom of God, emphasizing love, patience, and integrity. This means adopting pedagogical strategies that honor each student's dignity, promote collaborative learning, and encourage personal growth. By modeling these values, we create a classroom environment that is both nurturing and challenging, helping students to develop not only academically but also spiritually and morally.

Building a Reflective Practice

"Examine yourselves to see whether you are in the faith; test yourselves. Do you not realize that Christ Jesus is in you—unless, of course, you fail the test?" (2 Corinthians 13:5). Reflective practice is essential for continuous improvement and personal growth. As educators, we must regularly evaluate our teaching methods, relationships with students, and adherence to our educational philosophy. This self-examination helps us stay aligned with our faith and identify areas for development. By fostering a habit of reflection, we remain open to the Holy Spirit's guidance and become more effective in our ministry as educators.

Fostering Community Engagement

"You are the light of the world. A town built on a hill cannot be hidden. Neither do people light a lamp and put it under a bowl. Instead they put it on its stand, and it gives light to everyone in the house. In the same way, let your light shine before others, that they may see your good deeds and glorify your Father in heaven"

(Matthew 5:14-16). Engaging with the broader community is a vital aspect of implementing our educational philosophy. By actively participating in community service and outreach, we extend the impact of our faith beyond the classroom. This involvement not only benefits the community but also provides students with practical opportunities to live out their faith, reinforcing the lessons learned in school and fostering a lifelong commitment to service.

In Conclusion

"Therefore encourage one another and build each other up, just as in fact you are doing" (1 Thessalonians 5:11). As we conclude this chapter, let us be reminded of the importance of mutual support and encouragement in our journey as Christian educators. Implementing our educational philosophy requires dedication, reflection, and a collaborative spirit. By building each other up and working together, we create a strong, supportive community that can effectively nurture and inspire the next generation. Let us continue to strive towards excellence in our teaching, always seeking to glorify God through our words and deeds.

Writing Prompt for "Praxis: Implementing the Philosophy" Section of Your Philosophy of Christian Education Paper:

Develop a comprehensive plan for implementing your Christian educational philosophy. Focus on specific areas such as curriculum design, classroom management, and student assessment.

Chapter 10: Growth as a Disciplined Practice

A Journey of Continuous Improvement

"Being confident of this, that he who began a good work in you will carry it on to completion until the day of Christ Jesus" (Philippians 1:6). The path of a Christian educator is one of ongoing development and refinement. Our journey is not static but a dynamic process of growth, propelled by the assurance that God is continually working within us. Embracing this journey of continuous improvement means recognizing that each day presents new opportunities to learn, grow, and become more effective in our calling.

Embracing Reflection as a Catalyst for Growth

"Let us examine our ways and test them, and let us return to the Lord" (Lamentations 3:40). Reflection is a powerful tool for personal and professional growth. By regularly examining our actions, attitudes, and outcomes, we gain insights into areas where we can improve and align more closely with God's will. This reflective practice not only fosters self-awareness but also keeps us grounded in our faith, guiding us back to the Lord and His purposes for our lives and vocations.

The Evolving Nature of Our Educational Philosophy

"Do not conform to the pattern of this world, but be transformed by the renewing of your mind. Then you will be able to test and approve what God's will is—his good, pleasing and perfect will" (Romans 12:2). Our educational philosophy should not be rigid or static; it must evolve as we gain new insights and experiences. This transformation involves renewing our minds through continuous learning and adaptation. By staying open to new ideas and approaches, we ensure that our teaching remains relevant and impactful, aligned with God's good and perfect will.

Deepening Our Engagement with Students

"He is the one we proclaim, admonishing and teaching everyone with all wisdom, so that we may present everyone fully mature in Christ" (Colossians 1:28). Deepening our engagement with students involves more than just delivering content; it requires us to invest in their holistic development. By proclaiming Christ and teaching with wisdom, we guide students towards maturity in their faith and character. This deep engagement fosters meaningful relationships and creates a supportive learning environment where students feel valued and inspired to grow.

The Ripple Effect of Our Professional Growth

"Be diligent in these matters; give yourself wholly to them, so that everyone may see your progress. Watch your life and doctrine closely. Persevere in them, because if you do, you will save both yourself and your hearers" (1 Timothy 4:15-16). Our professional growth has a profound impact on those around us. As we diligently pursue excellence and integrity in our teaching, we set an example for our students and colleagues. This ripple effect extends beyond the classroom, influencing the broader community and advancing the Kingdom of God. By watching our life and doctrine closely, we ensure that our growth leads to positive, lasting change.

Looking Forward with Hope and Determination

"Therefore, since we are surrounded by such a great cloud of witnesses, let us throw off everything that hinders and the sin that so easily entangles. And let us run with perseverance the race marked out for us, fixing our eyes on Jesus, the pioneer and perfecter of faith" (Hebrews 12:1-2). As we look forward, we are inspired by the legacy of those who have gone before us. Their faith and perseverance encourage us to run our race with determination and hope. By fixing our eyes on Jesus, we stay focused on our ultimate goal and find the strength to overcome challenges. This forward-looking perspective keeps us motivated and aligned with our divine purpose.

In Conclusion

As we conclude this chapter, we are reminded of the importance of continual growth in both grace and knowledge found in the verse "But grow in the grace and knowledge of our Lord and Savior Jesus Christ. To him be glory both now and forever! Amen" (2 Peter 3:18). This disciplined practice of growth not only enhances our effectiveness as educators but also glorifies God. By committing to lifelong learning and spiritual development, we ensure that our teaching is infused with wisdom and love, guiding our students towards a deeper understanding of their faith and their role in God's plan.

Writing Prompt for "Spiritual Discipline: Growth as a Practice" Section of Your Philosophy of Christian Education Paper:

Envision your educational practice five years from now in the context of continuous growth and spiritual discipline. Outline the steps you will take to achieve this vision, incorporating the themes discussed in this book.

Sharing Your Philosophy

Writing Your Philosophy of Christian Education Paper

Now that you have completed the book and responded to each chapter's writing prompts, we invite you to compile your reflections into a cohesive paper. This paper should capture your journey through the book, highlighting key insights, personal reflections, and actionable steps for integrating Christian education principles into your practice.

Begin by reviewing your journal entries and identifying recurring themes or transformative insights. Organize your paper around these themes, providing examples from your responses to illustrate how your understanding and practice of Christian education have evolved.

Conclude with a personal action plan, outlining specific steps you intend to take to implement the principles discussed in the book. This paper will not only serve as a capstone to your reading experience but also as a roadmap for your continued growth as a Christian educator.

On the next few pages you will see an outline for the paper that will help you complete the writing of your philosophy paper.

My Philosophy of Christian Education

Your Name

Veritology: The Heart of Christian Education

Reflect on the core principles of Christian education and how they align with your personal educational philosophy. Discuss how these principles shape your approach to teaching and learning.

Theology: My Theological Perspective

Explore the theological foundations of your educational philosophy. How do biblical principles such as Colossians 1:16-17 influence your approach to teaching and curriculum design?

History: The Christian Narrative

Examine the historical role of Christianity in shaping education. Identify key figures and movements that have influenced Christian education and discuss their impact on your own educational practice.

Anthropology: A Christian Worldview

Analyze how a Christian worldview influences your understanding of humanity and the purpose of education. Compare this with other worldviews and discuss the implications for your teaching practice.

Ethics and Praxis: Practical Application

Detail how ethical principles derived from the Gospel guide your practical application of educational theories and practices. Provide examples from your teaching experience.

Philosophy and Ethics: Critical Engagement

Critically engage with contemporary educational philosophies and cultural issues through the lens of Christian ethics. Discuss how you integrate these insights into your teaching and interactions with students.

Unio Mystica: Reflection and Development

Reflect on your personal growth and development as a Christian educator. How do spiritual practices and self-reflection enhance your effectiveness in the classroom?

Sociology: Community and Service

Propose a community service initiative that integrates Christian sociological principles. Discuss how this initiative fosters a sense of community and service among your students.

Praxis: Implementing the Philosophy

Develop a comprehensive plan for implementing your Christian educational philosophy. Focus on specific areas such as curriculum design, classroom management, and student assessment.

Spiritual Discipline: Growth as a Practice

Envision your educational practice five years from now in the context of continuous growth and spiritual discipline. Outline the steps you will take to achieve this vision, incorporating the themes discussed in this book.

Dear Christian Educator,

I hope you are blessed by this wonderful opportunity to reflect on your perspectives and to articulate a vision for your classroom. I pray that God blesses your work and that it ultimately draws students into a closer relationship to Him.

Your brother in Christ, Dr. Ron Titus

Made in the USA
Columbia, SC
29 July 2024

7219581a-dd4b-46f3-8749-2888f1ce61c5R01